Vivi

From Dreams to *Awakening*!

From Dreams to *Awakening*!

Copyright © 2022 Vivian Larkin

ISBN 978-1-946683-42-7
Library of Congress Control Number 2022900829

Rapier Publishing Company
Dothan, Alabama 36301

www.rapierpublishing.com
Facebook: www.rapierpublishing@gmail.com
Twitter: rapierpublishing@rapierpub

Printed in the United States of America

All rights reserved under the International Copyright Law. Contents and/or cover may not be reproduced in whole or in part in any form without the consent of the Publisher or Author.

Book Cover Design: Daniel Ojedokun
Book Layout: Rapture Graphics
Cover Photo: Passion Photography

Rapier
PUBLISHING COMPANY

Dedication

This book is dedicated to the One who is responsible for it all! My Lord, Our Father, who touched and used hearts along the way to mold and shape me into the writer, the woman, and the author I am becoming today!

I magnify Jesus for this book and for the "Awakening" in me. I am fully persuaded that He has a plan and a purpose for you, His beloved, and through reading this book, may you encounter a glimpse of what He is saying to and through you because He wastes nothing! May you experience His presence and discover some truths you find beneficial along the way.

I thank every person that touched my life along the way, my husband, my parents, siblings, son, teachers, ministers, family, friends, and yes, even strangers. Let's continue, as much as lies within us to walk in love and walk toward the light!

Lord Jesus, in your name, let it be so that we never stop dreaming.

Let your awakening come now!

"And it shall come to pass in the last days, says God, That I will pour out of My Spirit on all flesh; Your sons and your daughters shall prophesy, Your young men shall see visions, Your old men shall dream dreams"
~Acts 2:17~
~Joel: 2: 28~

Vivian Larkin

From Dreams to Awakening!

A Glimpse

The warm light shimmered back and forth across my face. Dancing on my forehead. Kissing my cheeks. I was somewhere close to sleep but not close enough. With eyelids that were unwilling to part for more than a second, my eyes darted around the room shabbily investigating the source of the light. Aside from furniture & corners thinly veiled by darkness, I saw nothing but familiarity. I must've been dreaming. Hmph. I closed my eyes.

Little did I know that light - the one I could barely see - had been quietly and patiently surrounding me for quite some time. Then the subtleness stopped.

With the unbreakable focus of a wave coming to claim anything ready to leave the shore, the ground disappeared from under me. The light was pouring down on me, all the while washing over me, running through me. My eyes opened. And this time, I saw nothing but light--celestial, divine & graceful Light. This was unfamiliar.

Just like the wave rolling back to the sea gently cradling everything that surrendered, when the light pulled back, I went with it.

This is not a memoir, nor is it a story of fiction. Instead, it is an intimate testimony. Actually, it's two testimonies—one, a testimony of the relentless love God had for me before I surrendered; and another of His extraordinary love for me - His daughter Vivian - after I surrendered to Him.

This is what the Lord says, "I will guide you and teach you the way you should go. I will give you good advice and watch over you with love" (Psalms NIRV).

The following pages detail God's communication with me. Primarily through dreams, even so, you'll observe that God has been pursuing me in many ways, vying for my attention. Maybe you can relate.

How could I not see and understand that it was He? As my awakening continues to dawn, these questions are being answered. I am understanding things that were beyond my grasp just a short time ago.

I needed Him to guide me. I needed Him to be "Lord." Yet, I was oblivious to the need. So, it makes sense that I was just as blind to His never expiring invitation to lead.

I wasn't listening to the dreams or His word and didn't recognize Him. I failed to heed my loving Father's voice. It wasn't because I didn't want to hear God. To be blunt, I desperately wanted to hear from Him. But I am convinced today that I was blind and deaf to Him because my agenda was different from His.

My choices led me down paths he never intended for me. And yet, in the midst of me exercising free will, nothing I did was a surprise to God. And you can not surprise him either. None of us can.

As a child, I drifted between being a bit stubborn and downright unshakeable. Dancing, reading and writing were things I could live off of. Yet when I think about playing as a child- the way children just play - it was something I just didn't do.

Somewhere along the way, my innocence was stolen, and I became a victim. I responded by becoming good at protecting myself. Really good!

This need to protect myself was more than a shield. It ruled every single facet of my world. Every choice, every relationship, every move was under its destructive grip. I did not realize it at the time, but I was living in a prison of my own making.

I thought I knew what was best for me which only shored in a never ending flood of grief. The lies I told myself cost me dearly. They robbed me in every way thinkable, of relationship with God along with people relationships. Even after my surrender, surrounded by God's grace, I still deal with the consequences of leading my own life. If I can even call it that!

In Isaiah 48 the Lord says, "I am your God who teaches you what is best for you, who directs you in the way you should go. If only you had paid attention to my commands, your peace would have been like a river, your well being like the waves of the sea."

God speaks to me vividly! He speaks through dreams; through song and music; through the inner spirit, through ministers, through His Word. He even speaks through objects. Yes, stuff. Anyone and anything can be used by Him to bear witness to His Word. Us not hearing Him does not mean He's not speaking.

According to His Word, He is guiding us. And a good guide is close by at all times. This also means God is talking to us on a regular.

It took me a long time to get to the place of seeing and hearing him regularly. But it's a new day. The wiser me listens with expectation. I know He is constantly speaking to me, even when I am not hearing Him.

What about you? Are you aware that He is speaking to you? I applaud you if you do.

Many things about me have changed over the years. But some things remain fundamentally true—He still speaks to me through dreams and visions. Today, I'm sure they - my dreams and visions - are more. They were and are God's 'guideposts'. And I have had pretty specific guideposts that now, I've learned to recognize and take note of--without wasting time.

Guideposts that are presented to me in dreams & visions:

- This is the way, walk in it.
- Wait.
- Proceed with quickness.
- No.

Food for thought!

❖Is God pursuing you too? Relentlessly? How are you responding?

Because my dreams manifest results, they remind me of many recorded in the Word of God. For instance, in Genesis 37-50, it is recorded that Joseph had several dreams which he shared with his father and brethrens.

One dream he shared indicated that they would be bowing down to him. The brothers did not take well to that possibility, and they began to seek ways to get rid of the "dreamer". Most thought to kill him, but one interceded.

Eventually though, when he was just seventeen, the others succeeded in betraying him, removing him from the home and the land. Even so, they could not stop what God ordained.

After the betrayal, Joseph went from hardship to hardship. He was thrown in the pit, sold to foreigners and into slavery. He was finally falsely accused of attempted rape and thrown into prison. Even so, he continued to honor God and walk with integrity. As a result, God kept promoting him to favor regardless of his circumstances.

He interpreted several dreams which in due course (at age thirty), led him to interpret the Pharaoh's troubling dream. This interpretation opened the door to fulfillment of Joseph's dream wherein his brethren and father, more than twenty years after his dream, ultimately bowed before him.

I was told to document my dreams. I'm so grateful I obeyed the leading, which made it possible for me to share them today. I'm equally convinced, by Joseph's story, that not all dreams are meant to be shared at the time given.

There was this one time I had an intense dream I shared that I called "heart transplant". It was as intense as the title suggests. I felt remorse afterwards. But I naively divulged every detail despite them silently begging me to stop.

I now recognize this as one of those instances where God was showing me, "me". I'm beginning to understand more and more how doing things my way, instead of Jesus', allowed me to consider myself something that I was not. Basically, I was just immature and insensitive.

Something more to think about!

❖What are some things about yourself you consider to be good or virtuous but often leads to others being hurt or offended? How did you allow God to deal with these areas in your life?

So you ask how does God's messaging to me relate to you?

May you be moved to *reexamine* encounters and recurring themes you previously brushed off as nothing as anything but that.

It's my hope too that you become wise to your unique God moments so that you understand His messages to you; that you listen to Him and follow His lead. And please do not be as immovable as I was, especially not for as long as I was.

It's a bumpy road. I won't lie to you. But the road to awakening starts with making the choice to take it.

Reflection:

❖ Are you recognizing God's voice in your life, and will you choose to listen and consistently follow His lead?

Vivian Larkin

Your Reflections

_____

_____

_____

_____

_____

_____

_____

_____

_____

_____

_____

_____

_____

_____

_____

_____

_____

_____

_____

_____

_____

_____

From Dreams to *Awakening*!

Coming Next

One by One,
"The Dreams, the Awakening!"

Vivian Larkin

From Denial to Acceptance - a Metamorphosis

Between February and April 1998, dreamed Bill was in my life, then suddenly he was no longer there. The pain was so deep I couldn't stop crying. When I awakened, the pain was deep, and tears were flowing like a flood. It was so vivid, that I actually felt an unquenchable heart ache.

Did I listen with intent to understand God's message? I did not. Instead, I tried to outwit the dream. Though it was heavy on my mind, I did not record it. Nevertheless, I could not forget it.

Move forward a couple months to June 27, 1998, and Bill, (who lived in California at the time) and I (Georgia girl) got married without telling anyone. We started living together about ten months later (April 1999). We both had very severe childhood issues and those problems were extra baggage in the marriage causing much added conflict.

In my mind, I was Christ like, lovable, committed, self-sufficient and obedient. Unfortunately, there was a part of me completely hidden from "my" view. I was about to discover that truth. Although I didn't grasp it then, it all began after the 1999 wedding while on our honeymoon.

I became fanatical because Bill wanted to change our plans and watch the news about JFK Jr's plane crash instead of full focus on just us. Although we had just completed a full day of agreed upon activities, I was unwilling to be flexible.

In a country I had only been in for a few days, in a rage, I walked out the door in the dark of night. As selfish as I was being, God still protected me and I made it back to the timeshare a few hours later. Bill had searched for me to no avail and was upset but, unlike me, hid his feelings.

Yet back at home, about a month later, when I came home from work, he was gone and I was clueless as to why. My fairytale romance babe had skedaddled! My first reaction, "well, I have done nothing so if he can walk out like that for no reason, it's on him."

Bill's perspective today: After we started counseling months later, he learned that although he thought he had put his childhood behind him, it was controlling him. This was a turning point for him. In his childhood, even if he did something well, he says he was told it was wrong. So he learned to believe if things didn't go well, it was somehow his fault. He said this belief about himself caused him to jump into victim mode which contributed to his hasty, unannounced departure. As victim, he believed he was being pushed away.

It was several months after he left that the same pain I experienced in the dream came rushing in. It was unbearable just like in the dream. I cried uncontrollably. I'm thinking my husband has abandoned me.

I was confused. I was hurting and feeling betrayed. Then, it hit me--this is the second failing marriage, and I am the one common denominator.

Eventually, the pain and the Lord reminded me of the dream. It began a metamorphosis for me. At that point, I was ready for change.

I prayed, "Father, I have hurt so many people for so long." I confessed being tired of the heartache created when I'm in control. I admitted, I do not know what's best and I do not want to be in control anymore.

I repented in full surrender and committed to do it God's way. I acknowledged Him as creator and Lord whose plan far exceeds my own. I accepted that although man violated by trust, God would never do so. I believed for help to let go of the obsession with outcomes.

In that painful moment, I wanted to know my contribution to the problem. Not like the past, when I convinced myself the other person was always at fault. From that day, I decided I want to learn the lesson life wants to teach me. So I asked Him to teach me to do His will.

It became crystal clear to me that God had been my Saviour only. I was lord...which resulted in lukewarm Christianity. I tried to control. I was self-righteous, judgmental, argumentative, insecure, insensitive and uncompromising (my way was the only correct way).

I had what I have recently learned to be a "god complex." Meaning, I had a major attitude and an "ugly" personality. Seeing and accepting responsibility for this truth about myself was instrumental for change.

Be sure, change did not happen instantly, as a matter of fact, God is still helping me become who He wants me to be. I am a continual work in progress.

In the year 2000, gradually God began to shed more light on me. I was saddened by what I saw and what I saw was what others close to me had been seeing all along and choosing to tolerate. My husband though, who had experienced his own traumatic childhood, chose not to tolerate this disrespectful attitude.

This is what the Lord says in Rev 3 about who I was, "I know your deeds, that you are neither cold nor hot. I wish you were either one or the other! So, because you are lukewarm—neither hot nor cold—I am about to spit you out of my mouth."

The dream I had hoped to avoid was used by God to initiate a much needed change in me (from "lukewarm" to devoted) so I would become a vessel He could use.

Over time, I came to realize why lukewarm is the worst state of a soul; and also how when we are fully committed, devoted to and submitted to His Lordship, God can use me or you to be a blessing to ourselves and others.

The change in me began to surface as change in my relationships for the better. Blessed is the one who heeds wisdom's instruction (Proverbs 29:18).

Don't get me wrong, I still get to constantly choose to die to self because if I take my eyes off Jesus too long and start thinking of me, I shift to the wrong lane, I try to self-protect.

More thought provoking ponders!

❖ Are you growing, changing for the better consistently? Or, like I was, are you lukewarm and clueless about it?

❖ How do you treat others when things don't go your way? Hopefully, better than I did.

❖ Would you say that God truly has your heart?

From Lukewarm to Devotion – the Snake – May 26, 1999

Seems lukewarm can be deceptive. As I stated earlier, I was in denial about the state of my soul. But the Lord opened my understanding to the fact that I was not the Christian I thought myself to me.

In this dream, Bill told me he saw a snake. I looked around and saw the snake under a bush. Next thing I knew, the snake was on my head. Fearfully, I eased backward toward Bill until he could knock it off my head. I awakened.

It appears the Lord was letting me know that Bill saw the hypocrisy before I had a clue about my true spiritual state. It was a warning, yet, I failed to acknowledge and take heed at the time.

Before Bill and I married, a true Christian friend counseled me that God would require more of me since I was professing Christianity. Even so, my listening was dull and I had to learn that lesson the hard way.

Today I am reminded on a regular, that the cost of rebellion and disobedience is steep so I now choose consciously to be intentional in obedience. Still miss it sometimes, but my heart says obey!!!

Time for thinking about it!

❖ Have you had any indication from the Father that

your relationship with Him breaks His heart by giving others the wrong impression of who He is?

❖ What will you do with that knowledge?
❖ Will you choose to yield?

From Dreams to *Awakening*!

Your Reflections

From Child to Adult much too soon, from darkness to light - Reaching Hand

November 25, 2002. This vision entailed walking through what appeared to be a beautiful home. I said appeared because I sensed unseen darkness there. Once out the door, I crossed rough spots in the yard.

Then 'we' climbed a steep hill. Almost near the top, for support, I grabbed a tree branch growing out the side of the hill. Suddenly, a man was holding the branch in His hand, and He was reaching down to us, saying grab hold.

Immediately upon awakening, I sensed it was the Lord helping us up the side of the hill. But I couldn't remember who the other person was. I wrote near the dream, thoughts of Larry.

Larry is my firstborn. We started out together in the big city of Atlanta when I was just seventeen. Subsequently, mom convinced me to bring him to her. Later, I joined the military and left him with mom again while I went overseas. Sometimes later, he stayed with my big sister Flo.

When I returned a few years later, I was a new Christian but blind to the fact that I was 'lord' over me. I got us a house but failed to build a home. And I didn't demonstrate a foundation of faith for him to follow. I focused on provision, rather than on spending quality time and training him properly.

I lacked supporting him at his ball games. As well, I argued with my first husband, Joseph all the time. God puts it this way, "An angry person stirs up conflict, and a hot tempered person commits many sins". There was a lot of screaming and hollering (mostly initiated by me) and I exhibited attitude far too often. Once, while yelling, Larry came downstairs and asked, "Can't you guys ever talk without screaming"?

Regrettably, I did not realize my inability to communicate effectively could create a high level of instability for him. I did not understand then, that words have power either for life or death. And I did not realize we must choose our words carefully, and especially keeping them to a minimum when angry.

I failed at giving most of the important things a child needs, a loving and peaceful home, hugs, affirmation, quality time and attention. Larry suffered as a result. I see that now. I have since apologized, but still miss that heart-to-heart love connection.

My hope is that this dream indicates, in spite of the unseen darkness in the home (most likely pride in me then, and maybe some in him now), God reached out, has pursued us and is helping us both reach the level of closeness He ordained. In a second dream later about connection, this hope is confirmed.

First Real Glimpse at Childhood Related Pivots

When Bill and I had individual counseling with

Rosalyn in early 2000, in relation to my childhood, she would say at each session that it was not my fault, I was a child. I don't need to carry shame and guilt. I didn't take it to heart though.

I assumed she should be talking about the marriage issues, not my childhood. Nonetheless, one day she said those words and they resonated! I began to believe. She instantly recognized that I needed to identify the lies I believed about myself. As a child, I had taken on the sins of the molester, believing it was my fault. Although belief in that lie had been with me for a long, long time, truth is "it was NOT my fault."

Now I know I also needed to accept responsibility for my own disobedience and sins! I did not have this revelation during Larry's childhood. No, I was not responsible for the violation. Yet, I was the one who chose the road to single parenting. I was equally responsible for loving and for training that child in the way God would have him to go, yet I did a botched job with that too.

Do my failures make me a bad person? Absolutely not! Nor do yours. I, like all of us, am a product of life experiences and my environment. I was a person who needed a personal relationship with Jesus as Lord and Savior.

Something else for thought!

❖ What lie do you believe?

From Dreams to *Awakening*!

❖ Why not dissect it with Truth?

From Controlling to Letting Go, from obstacle to breakthrough - New Driver

Who is driving in your life? Is it you? How about a significant other? Is it mom or dad? Is it past traumas? How often do you stop to reflect on the results? Are you arriving at the destination you thought you would reach? Or, like me, have you ended in predicaments you hoped to avoid?

My life, like the car in this upcoming dream, had been out of control for many years. Most of the time, I thought I needed to make things happen, which resulted in a merry-go-round effect.

Although it would end in disaster, I couldn't and wouldn't relinquish control. Instead, I would try again, maybe slightly different. Doing the same things, expecting different results is considered insanity. That was me in action.

In the dream of **June 14, 1998,** I hurt my heel and someone else had a bloody hole in their hand. I went for help and ended up in my car. The car was out of control and being swept into a river. I closed my eyes. I opened them only after the car stopped moving. I was no longer driving but in the passenger seat. I said forget the car. I need to get out of here.

As I thought to get out, the car began moving back out of the river. It backed unto the shoreline. When it stopped, I applied the parking brake. Then I saw the river was not water, but a bed of large rocks and boulders. As I stared, the car began moving backward again, up to the top of an embankment.

I went to the person and told them God had performed a miracle. I explained I had not gotten help and they showed me that they had been healed; God had performed a miracle for them too. Then I realized I too had received healing.

A friend's insight – Satan sought to drown or destroy me, to swallow me up, but God performed a miraculous deliverance. When I recognized what was happening, I applied the brakes--made an attempt to refrain.

At first, I was seeking help through worldly ways. The power of the cross and its representation was signified by the hand, the bruised heel. God performed a mighty deliverance once I released control.

As I began to see this 1998 vision unfold in my marriage in 2020, I recognized and said as long as I was driving, I was heading into troublesome, hard places. But it wasn't just related to the marriage, it was my life in my hands. After I applied brakes or tried to refrain from doing it my way, then God's miracle working power started revealing itself.

When I let go of the wheel and He took control, the car stopped. God accomplishes what we can not do. He works in ways we can not understand.

We have a part to play in the unfolding of our lives and God has a role to play. My biggest problem was that I was trying to do God's work. God's role is His alone and He will not give His glory to us. My role (our role) is to partner with God. Are you dear reader a partner with God or like I was, trying to play God?

The awakening and breakthrough today, I am seeing the light and also the powerful hand of God moving in my life. Nonetheless, when I get in survival mode and put self first, I find myself wanting to take control again. Sometimes it's easier than others but when He reminds me of the wheel in my hands versus the wheel in His, I surrender.

God is also speaking to you, my friend. If you are young, start listening now. If you are older like me, start listening now. With God in control, things flow so much better. Are there challenges? Yes, there are.

However, there is a peace in knowing He either ordains it or permits it. In either situation, He has a purpose. I know the plans I have for you, says the Lord; plans to prosper you and not to harm you.

Those who trust in themselves are fools, {like I was} but those who walk in wisdom are kept safe. See Proverbs 28

Something for thought!

❖ Again, whose the driver of your life?

From Dreams to *Awakening*!

Your Reflections

Vivian Larkin

From Darkness to Light – A Much Needed Awakening (Perfectionist)

In this December 1990 dream, my manager was leaving for California. I was getting my previous manager back. I was very sad. I awakened very distraught and in tears.

God had used my previous manager to point out the perfectionist in me. I had not realized the effect being one had on others until I worked with one. It was very frustrating; it was as if I could do nothing to his satisfaction. In reality, I was relieved that he had moved on to another position. Yet, in this dream, he was returning. This brought me great sadness. An awakening in itself!

Prior to working with Mr. C, I was so over the top with everyone, especially those in my own household. I thought I was just going the extra mile but I was in darkness. I am grateful the Lord allowed me to work with him long enough to realize AND know firsthand the negative and draining affect a perfectionist has on those who are close to them.

Having that type of impact on others is not something that brings glory to the Father. It actually does the opposite. It helps the enemy suck life out of people. To this day, with His help, I do my best to stay away from perfectionism.

Admittedly, even after the Mr. C. ordeal, the

perfectionist spirit was prevalent in me, and it contributed to troubled waters in both marriages. The Word declares "a wise woman builds her house, but the foolish tears it down with her hands". That foolish woman was me. It took years before I began yielding to God, which was and is the help I needed to modify my behavior.

Yes, we are to give life our best shot, but we also need to know when it's time to pull up and leave the outcome to God.

How am I doing? I'd like to believe I am doing better. However, one day when I finished the yard, my granddaughter told me, "you know you are borderline perfectionist, right? My guess, she saw some essence of that trait still in me.

Something to reflect on!
❖ Is being a perfectionist an issue you face?

❖ If you live with one, how are you communicating the impact it has on you?

From bondage to freedom - Choose this day, who you will serve

Have you ever chosen to make someone else happy, yet compromise your walk with the Father? Lord knows, I have. Fear of man will prove to be a snare, but whoever trusts in the Lord is kept safe.

In this dream on **January 31, 1985**, I was saying, "they worship the creature more than the creator; you must serve God, not man". I awakened. Then, went back to sleep and dreamed the same thing again. Out of the mouths of two or three witnesses, shall every word be established.

Considering I recommitted my life to Jesus in the late seventies, I see now, He was telling me I was still making some bad choices. I had many opportunities to serve God over man, and I failed miserably. I was a people pleaser—either pleasing myself or someone else over honoring God.

Today I know I missed the warning from this dream because my heart wasn't fully committed. Years after this dream and many hard places, I have started learning to serve God first.

For instance, in 2018, a couple of friends, on separate occasions, told me Matthew 19 says it's okay to divorce. A few years before their advice, I tried to end the relationship with Bill by asking him to finish what he started and file for divorce. I committed to foot the cost.

I was trying to circumvent my promise to God in an around about way. God did not endorse that plan.

While listening to them, I was reminded again that I promised God I would receive that what He has joined together is no longer twain, but one flesh. So I knew to disregard their advice. Although I was willing to take the chance, I was hopeful it didn't mean living without the companionship of a husband for the rest of my life.

Since I had become well aware, that my choice to disobey God's earlier warning to wait, came with consequences, the thought of adding more bad results did not appeal to me. I prayed for forgiveness and grace to experience marriage fellowship, yet I could not be sure how God would answer.

Conversely, I had already divorced my first husband, Joseph—twice by that time. So, I am not claiming sainthood, just a choice in obedience.

With God, we get to choose. It's up to us whether we choose to follow Him fully or as James puts it, (and like I was for many years) be like a wave in the sea that is up and down in our Christianity (James 1:6).

Now, after more than twenty years of separateness, I am learning to unite with my husband and fight for what God has for us. Had I listened to the voice of the enemy, telling me what I wanted to hear, we could've been history. Too often I did listen to the wrong voice and it always cost dearly. The result may have been temporary pleasure, but in the end, I lost more than I gained.

Think about this!

❖ Have you been tempted to sway from what you know God is saying to you?

❖ Proverbs warns, it's wise to calculate the cost beforehand. Have you counted the cost of your choice?

From Dreams to *Awakening*!

Your Reflections

_____

_____

_____

_____

_____

_____

_____

_____

_____

_____

_____

_____

_____

_____

_____

_____

_____

_____

_____

_____

_____

_____

Vivian Larkin

From Idol Worship to Reverential Fear of God - The House Fire

Are there idols in your life? Do you start your day with anything other than time with the Father—giving Him the first fruit? Are you committed to God BUT you compromise and rationalize the scripture when it comes to a certain person or thing? Do you say, "I know what the Word says, but...?" I did.

On August 30, 1999, I dreamed there was a fire in our home (house looked unfamiliar). Fire began downstairs (downstairs looked familiar). I got directions to the fire department. When I arrived and was asking for help, I looked about to see the smoke very thick and black.

When we got back to the property, it was still standing. So I started trying to decide what to save from the fire. At that point, we realized the fire was still contained downstairs.

I looked downstairs. Fire was burning but nothing consumed. However, two statues had fallen. After I awakened, I thought the dream may be indicating two idols in my life that needs to bow before the throne of God.

I recognized that one idol was my husband. I had put him before God. When God said not to marry, I kept begging until I thought He changed His mind. Now I know He simply did not override my "free" will.

When I recently shared this dream with Bill, he indicated that he thinks the second idol was me because likewise, he had put me on a pedestal. Yet, I am sure the second idol was pride in me. Back then, I just had to have things my way, and I was a know it all too.

This dream was 1999. And in 2010, the Lord spoke to me from Rev 21 saying "it is done." I felt my mind knew what it meant. Problem was, I had a strong desire to hear more of what it was saying. Those three words stuck with me and I asked consistently, Lord, what does that mean?

I don't recall how long it took, but one day when I asked the question, I heard very clearly, "everything in life is already done when you do life God's way."

"Everything in life is already done when I do life God's way."

This was a light-bulb moment. I don't have to be in control and it won't always go according to my plan BUT it will always go according to His plan because He sees the end from the beginning and He has already won victory for us.

In light of this rhema word, I realize that God has a fulfilling purpose for my life and I simply need to obey Him. Unlike before when I had to control the situation, this revelation reminds and guides me when I start hearing the lie that *self-sufficiency* needs to kick in. It helps to finally recognize that I really don't like the company it keeps...

My husband and I are each painfully seeing and acknowledging our individual flaws and failures. And at a pace sufficient for the individual, we are working to become our best selves.

Do you or have you ever had an issue with idols-- pride, a person, or any other thing that had more value to you than God? Your answer requires careful thought.

I say careful thought because I know had I been asked this question when my desire to marry Bill was more important than God's desire for me to wait, I would have justified that I was not putting him ahead of my love for God. Denial or not, that is exactly what I did and that disobedience came with a high price!

Thinking Time:

❖ Have you found anything or anyone who loves you like Jesus?

From Miscommunication to Conflict Resolution – from Fear to Faith,

May 1, 2020: Dreamed twice. Bill was honoring the marriage covenant, honoring God; then I sensed or saw in the spirit that God was blessing, moving in the situation. This dream came a few months before we learned how to fight fair and communicate with conflict resolution in mind.

When God sent this dream, I had begun to listen more intently for His voice. Moreover, I had begun to ride on His momentum. Still, at some points with my marriage the first few months, my flesh was kicking and screaming. My focus leaned toward circumstances. As a result, insecurity and fear set in for us both.

My devotion to God was going through a major test because there was also fear that as I humbled myself before God, I would be taken advantage of. Would I yield my will to God or pull back? I struggled. Bill and I could not discuss my fears, nor his, without conflict, so eventually, we both pulled back.

There was fear that he was attempting to hold on to his single lifestyle while saying we are leaving the past behind and beginning again as one. After he sent what he considered an innocent birthday message to one of his "friends", I confronted him about keeping the past in the present.

He stood his ground of innocence. I stood my ground

of refusing to continue to be the "other woman" in my own marriage. We each made ourselves the victim, then abruptly ended the reconciliation. Our families gave up on us long ago. We were finally doing the same.

I had become a realist by then. I recognized our impossibility was God's possibility, for with God all things are possible. And, I also knew God was not going to force either of us to do anything against our own will.

Since we only communicated frustrations and had no reliable tools to communicate our fears and feelings, we quit. We were doing the same things, expecting different results. So, we actually gave up on ever being together.

It was at that point, I began to see God move in the relationship. Today, Bill and I are **working at and growing into** a deeper respect, trust, and honor of each other and the marriage. But we began to experience this growth ONLY AFTER complete surrender.

God had explicitly told me to shut my mouth and He would speak to Bill. Yes, that was difficult, until He reminded me of the high cost of disobedience. After that reminder, I just continued in a pity party with God all day.

Although Bill called, I obeyed God. On one call, he left a voicemail saying if you don't call me, I'm coming over. I was hoping he would come. A few hours later, he showed up.

As we discuss it NOW, he indicates that he was impelled to come, that he felt he had no other choice. What I see is, the Lord was ready to do a new thing and we both had to relinquish control before He could do His best work! He was about to uproot over twenty years of misunderstandings.

Anyway, when Bill arrived, he insisted I tell him why I was so upset and crying. I told him again, God said He would tell you. Bill's sarcastic response was, "well, I didn't get the call." Shortly thereafter, he started blurting out things I did that hurt or offended him more than twenty years earlier.

Some I remembered, some I was clueless about. When he mentioned the honeymoon, I knew exactly what he was talking about because the drama I had created was unforgettable for me too. At the end, Bill said, "I can't believe I told you that. He must have spoken to me."

After a few hours of quiet closeness, we decided to part ways forever again. What the Lord had done was shed light on the root of Bill's fears in the relationship, which were instrumental in feeding my own fears. The statements gave us both something to think about.

Bill says he had an exhale moment enroute home. Fast forward a day and Bill was hurting from having those roots of bitterness dug up and exposed. The Lord ministered to me that it's no longer about Bill and me, it's about the image of God Bill had seen through me years earlier (hypocrisy) and it's about his salvation.

I was instructed in a step by step walk of humility. Since pleasing God had become more important to me than having my own way, I obeyed. I called with a sincere apology that was not accepted.

The Lord led me through several more steps until it ended in what I labeled "self mockery". Even so, I knew I had to resist rebellion (which was telling me not to humiliate myself) and I had to obey the Lord.

That obedience prompted a call to Bill from the west coast. A few days later, as a result of the call, Bill and I had a meaningful conversation and apology. Our dialogue was no longer superficial, but seemed to have content and depth.

Thinking it's all over, I chose counseling in an effort to move on with life "without" Bill. When I shared my plans, he asked if he could go too.

More on Bill's perspective: He says he thought it was over for us. Yet he felt it important for the counselor to hear both perspectives. When I mentioned it, she agreed that it was a splendid idea.

We had a few individual and some couple therapy. Our counselor, Sophia Gethers provided relationship conflict resolution and fair fighting tools as homework assignments. It changed the course.

After about three months, she told us to continue to work on communicating with each other and everything else would fall into place. Then she pushed us out the nest per se, saying we know how to contact her IF we need her.

There is much, much residue in our relationship as a result of twenty years of division, disorder and bad choices. I am constantly reminded, "be quiet, I will speak to him". I am equally reminded that we are to forgive, choose to resolve conflict and choose to work together for us.

We are to refrain from trying to change each other because free-will is at play. Even God can't change us if we don't want to be changed. There must first be a willing mind.

We have wasted enough time, energy and resources, but God doesn't even waste our mess-ups. God has purpose in everything He ordains as well as everything He allows.

Through our messed up relationship, God has allowed many opportunities for me to learn how to love unconditionally AND I admit, I do not always pass the test the first time but I yearn to please Him and that helps. I know that when the Lord is pleased, I am doing the right thing toward my husband and others.

Bill and I certainly do not have it all together. Not by a long shot. But I choose to believe we are both banding together to receive all that God has for us. God's been speaking through everything of late, even ceramic elephants. Through those magnificent animals, I heard, "speak no evil, and see no evil".

The Lord also said to me, learn to embrace what I am bringing and release what I am removing. The key has always been obedience. Yet, in the past through my self-protect role, I sported half-hearted obedience like a trophy. With God, we either obey or disobey. In His light, I now see my half-heartedness was costly disobedience.

There are still times when I don't like my husband as I am sure there are times when he doesn't like me. Nevertheless, I am reminded that I love him, that he loves me, and that I am not giving up on us. God is guiding me through this dream to put my expectation in Him to experience the marriage He ordains.

Time for Thought!

❖ How do you resolve conflict?

❖ What is God bringing into your life and asking you to embrace?

❖ What is He removing from your life? Are you releasing?

From Dreams to *Awakening*!

Your Reflections

_____

_____

_____

_____

_____

_____

_____

_____

_____

_____

_____

_____

_____

_____

_____

_____

_____

_____

_____

_____

_____

_____

_____

Vivian Larkin

From Fear to Faith, From Dislike to Love - Déjá Vu Dream, March 7, 1986

We were hugging, holding hands and walking. The love felt strong. It caused me to fear allowing myself to love so deeply. As I was thinking to pull back, I heard a voice saying, "go ahead and love him, then you will know how to love others."

I didn't recognize him as someone I knew, and he was taller. We hugged a lot. It was just pure love, no sex in mind or thought. I assumed the tallness meant I was looking up to him.

When I joined Bill in Vegas in November 1997, I remember telling him it felt like déjá vu. I questioned that feeling because I had never been there before and didn't know him, considering we had only met two months earlier.

Bill's Perspective - as we talked after a football game, I was telling him about a planned solo trip to Vegas to see the lights. He volunteered to meet me there which I thought was cool. Today, he tells me he wanted to protect me because he thought a country girl like me was a bit naive.

Ten years later, in December 2007 I was led to go through my journals and compile all dreams. Upon reading this dream, I understood the déjá vu experience for the first time. However, by that time, although I still loved him and we had tried several unsuccessful attempts at reconciliation, Bill and I were separated. He had moved on.

As God instructed in this dream, over the last few decades, I've started learning to reverence and love Him. This, in turn, is pulling me further away from the god-complex as I intentionally surrender and yield my will to His consistently.

The Awakening--the person I detested most in life was me (although I did not see it, it was very much present). God is helping me learn to be at peace with who I am and who I am becoming. He's showing me how to love me and others just the way we are (character flaws and shortcomings too). He's teaching me over and over again, to recognize we are all a work in progress.

Now I know that before, my strongest desire was to please me—the person I sub-consciously ostracized. Even so, I put up a good masquerade for most. Those closest to us normally see the real us in spite of our pretense.

Today, I don't need an act and I'm grateful for the much needed contrast. It's all about pleasing God. He knows me just the way I am, better than I know myself YET He loves me unconditionally. What I needed all along was Gods' perspective, not a counterfeit. Then I needed to keep walking toward the light.

I also recognize that God revealed through this dream twelve years before I met Bill that I would choose the way of Balaam (Numbers 22-24). When I asked about marrying Bill I felt strongly that God said it was not the time.

Now I know God didn't have Bill's heart, nor did God have my heart. But like Balaam I kept going back until I felt the lead to go ahead as described in 2 Peter 2:15. "They have left the straight way and wandered off to follow the way of Balaam...who loved the wages of wickedness".

The Lord said to me, "I am the Lord your God, who teaches you what is best for you, who directs you in the way you should go. If only you had paid attention to my commands, your peace would have been like a river, and your well being like the waves of the sea..." (Isa 48:17-18).

Anytime I have chosen my way over God's way, I have chosen the way of wickedness. I realize God didn't change His mind, and by the same token, He was not going to override my free will. Nonetheless, although I betrayed Him, and went through hell and back, He has worked much good and continues to work much good out of the situation.

God doesn't waste anything. As the awakening continues to dawn, it came to me that God chose to use my disobedience to teach me to love Him. Similarly, I am learning God's order for love. He, then me, then others as I love myself.

Time for Reflection:

❖ Where has God said no or wait in your life and you disregarded it?

❖ How are those circumstances treating you at this time?

From Pride to Humility - Woman of Scorn in contrast to One of Character

This woman of scorn was me in full force in my first marriage. Did I see it? No. Did I recognize after the dream? No. I now know I was on my own path and I didn't tune in to what God was saying, how He was attempting to direct me.

In December 1990, I dreamt God was teaching me the character of a woman who honors God by earning and maintaining her husband's respect in contrast to the woman who dishonors God, her true self and her husband.

In addition, He reveals some unpleasant associated consequences of being obstinate. Please pay particular attention if you have this foolish woman character flaw. Over the years since, God has shown me much about her in Proverbs. It truly awakened the need for change in me.

We were at a feast in this dream. I sat at the end of the table even though my husband asked me not to. He said, there will be no food there. As he had warned, the food was all gone before it reached me. I was trying to find food, everyone else was leaving. I got upset when I saw that he was leaving too.

In the next scene, he was with a lady who was of a quiet spirit. He provided her with food and shelter. I became resentful and upset.

Later the Lord ministered a scriptural message shared by a friend. Good things right at my fingertips but sin withheld them from me (Jerermiah 5:25). In this case it was the prideful me. My husband didn't care for her.

The woman who honors God and spouse displays a quiet spirit, humble, caring – at peace attitude (1 Peter 3); husbands love and provide for this type woman. He supplies her needs, beautifies her home. (Jeremiah 6:16; Prov 28:10). Thus, now that God has my attention, He continues teaching me how to honor He and my husband and find rest for my soul at the same time. Still a process though, still a process.

With each day in marriage, comes the choice to be a woman of character or a woman of dishonor. May I continually be reminded of this dream and choose to bring glory to God by becoming the wife He created me to become, the wife my husband needs; the wife I want to be.

I missed it with Joseph, and with the first years of marriage to Bill. In the present, with a mindset to please God, I am choosing to realize the benefits of being a honorable wife far outweigh the temporary pain of required discipline.

Have you chosen to honor when what you really wanted to do was give your mate a mouthful? I have not arrived. I struggle with this, especially when I start looking at "conditions", or when I do not like my mate.

Yet, I know God wants to love "unconditionally" through me at all times. So, I get to be deliberate in making the right choice here, moment by moment, day by day.

Pride doesn't have a gender though. This message was to me; still honor in marriage goes both ways—husbands to love their wives as themselves, wives to respect our husbands. How are you doing with this as a spouse?

If you want to know how I am doing, I prefer you ask my husband!

Reflection Time:

❖ Are you humble or prideful?

From Dreams to *Awakening*!

Your Reflections

_____

_____

_____

_____

_____

_____

_____

_____

_____

_____

_____

_____

_____

_____

_____

_____

_____

_____

_____

_____

_____

_____

_____

Vivian Larkin

From Crooked to Straight, From Judge to Witness - the Witness of Salvation

In the dream of June 24, 2000, I drove across an ocean and saw dad. The bridge I rode across just before reaching dad had clear water beneath it.

As I was sharing this dream with my husband, I received a call from my brother Jimmy. He was calling to thank me for witnessing to dad while he was alive. This was God speaking confirmation as I was telling the dream and the story of how God blessed me to realize my love for dad.

Dad had been in an automobile accident a few years earlier and wasn't expected to survive. It was at that point, the bitterness I felt toward him dissolved and I hoped for a chance to show my love to him.

The Lord granted that request and I spent the next few years appreciating dad for who he was, not who I wanted him to be.

For years, I had judged and thought I hated dad for his shortcomings as a husband. That crooked path in me was NOT from God. Satan knew God was going to use me to plant the seed for dad's salvation and had I remained aloof, I would have missed that opportunity.

I am reminded of the dream the Lord gave Israel's enemies in Judges 7:13-25. Gideon was skeptical about going against this mass army that covered the ground like locust because God had reduced Gideon's troops to 300 men.

The Lord said to Gideon, get up, go down against the camp, because I am going to give it into your hands. If you are afraid to attack, go down…and listen to what they are saying. Afterward, you will be encouraged to attack.

So Gideon and his servant went near the camp. Gideon arrived just as a man was telling a friend his dream. "I had a dream, he was saying. A round loaf of barley bread came tumbling into the Midianite camp. It struck the tent with such force that the tent overturned and collapsed." His friend responded, "This can be nothing other than the sword of Gideon. God has given the Midianites and the whole camp into his hands."

When Gideon heard the dream and its interpretation, he bowed down and worshipped. Then he and his men went to the Midianite camp where the Midianites turned on each other with their swords or fled. Thus the Lord defeated the enemy.

I shared Gideon's experience here to say when we do life God's way, the enemy is ALWAYS defeated. That's exactly what God did when I forgave my dad for being human and in need of a savior, just like me.

Judging did nothing for my relationship with dad except steal it from me. I am no better than he or anyone else for that matter. I have made many poor choices in men. I was a foolish woman as a wife (twice). I not only had a negative affect on husbands, but on my child as well. And we won't even mention extended family here.

Please rethink your animosity against an imperfect loved one and where possible, let God heal you and heal the relationship. Let me put a clarifier here. God commands us to forgive so we are released from the tormentors. I am not asking you to condone "abuse" of any kind. Do not return to an abusive relationship (whether physical, verbal, or sexual) as a result of these writings.

Forgiveness doesn't mean the other person didn't cause us pain, it means we release right to be judge and vindicator. That's God's job. And who among us doesn't have something for which we need to be forgiven. The Word declares we are to forgive, and God will forgive us. And if we say we love God but hate our brethren, the love of God is not in us. For abusers, forgive them and love them from a distance.

Forgiveness starts a process of releasing the baggage so we are lighter going forward with our lives. May the Lord teach us to number our days that we may gain a heart of wisdom.

Time for Reflection:

❖ He that is without sin, let him cast the first stone! Will that be you?

From Sickness to Deliverance - Preparation for Dad's Transition

The Lord prepared me for dad's transition through a comforting dream on **September 8, 1984** (a few days before dad passed). Dreamed I went to see dad at the nursing home, and he met me at the door. He looked great, full flesh and everything. He said to me, "I am alright, I am leaving." I felt instant relief.

It was later in the day when it dawned on me that dad was about to transition. Unstoppable tears started flowing down my cheeks. Back at home, I decided to make him a gospel tape and go stay with him. Since I was into contemporary gospel, it took a long time to listen to and select ole time gospel.

My first husband, Joseph asked me to wait until morning rather than go down at night. I did. We didn't have cell phones and mom called our home but I was already on the road. I arrived at the nursing home about an hour after dad passed.

I believe that maybe it is possible; dad met me at the door of the nursing home that morning. He had received his deliverance from God. He was leaving this earthly realm. No more aches and pain, no more agony from the cancer, nor the surgery. He was finally free of this mortal body, free of suffering.

Grateful that God's preparation helped me be strong for others, including mom, as we grieved dad's departure. Because He's a loving God, I feel sure He has prepared you for loss too. Can you think of an instance?

By the same token, can you see why it is so very important to love those close to us while it is called today? Regardless of how we think about it, tomorrow is not promised. Our days are numbered for sure.

❖ Is the reason for your separation from a loved one really worth losing the time you could still be enjoying together?

❖ If not, be the bigger person, apologize even if you feel you were wronged.

You will be surprised at the doors that will begin to open before you from just this one simple act of kindness. I urge you to seek God about the relationship. Listen to His advice. And make the right move today!

From Dreams to *Awakening*!

Your Reflections

_____

_____

_____

_____

_____

_____

_____

_____

_____

_____

_____

_____

_____

_____

_____

_____

_____

_____

_____

_____

_____

_____

_____

_____

Vivian Larkin

From a Heart of Stone to a Heart of Flesh (Heart Transplant)

On **December 10, 2013**, I dreamed my husband was having a heart transplant. Only he was someone I did not recognize. After the surgery, we went to my husband's house (both Bill, the heart transplant guy and me). He wanted to go out back and sit on the patio but the sprinkler was on so Bill (the gentleman) turned the sprinkler off while the new guy and I went upstairs to see the house.

I awakened and in my spirit I heard: "Wait on the Lord, be of good courage, and "write the vision, make it plain, for it will come to pass at the time appointed."

Sometime later, as I continued to ponder and question the Lord about the meaning, He took me to Ezekiel "I will give them an undivided heart and put a new spirit in them; I will remove from them their heart of stone and give them a heart of flesh. They will follow my decrees and be careful to keep my laws. They will be my people, and I will be their God."

Move forward to the awareness of 2020 (seven years later). The man who is now my husband, still Bill the gentleman, but a man I've not known before. I see a new man with a heart that's beginning to hear God and a willingness to honor our marriage covenant. It's a process too!

But God isn't just changing Bill's heart, He's changing

mine as well. I recognize that God was preparing each of us for a "new heart" to replace the heart of stone erected as children and carried into our adulthood and marriage. In His light, we see light as we are able to receive!

It's about "us" now with God as Lord. No more driving for me. God is head and He has an order. With His help, I humble myself before He and my husband as He allows more and more opportunities for me to learn to be more flexible. This results in Bill and I communicating more and fighting fairly, most of the time. Even so, there are still rough edges on either of us and they still require discretion.

I am seeing and learning that a heart of flesh feels and gives love, forgives, leans into humility, is peaceful, submissive—doesn't have to have it's own way but surrenders to what's best for the whole. It has expectations that as it yields itself to the ways of God, God will protect, provide and bring healing. For me to surrender during the tests, I need to pray for the Holy Spirit to help me to honor God.

From experience, I can say a heart of stone can exhibit any of these awful traits at any given time. When it feels a need to protect itself, it can be cold; other times, it is prideful (looks down it's nose at other's faults while minimizing it's own); dishonors others, acts unseemly; is easily angered, wants things that makes it happy, even at the expense of hurting others, unforgiving, and so on.

Time for Thought!

❖ Is God speaking to you about change?

❖ How are you responding? Your answer will tell you if He has your heart.

From Lies to Truth; From Bondage to Freedom - From Defender to Supporter

Are there any people in this life that have never suffered trauma of some kind? Are you one of them? I am not. Nevertheless, we look at each other, put on smiling faces and say all is well. But is it really?

I finally realize that although we cloak past ordeals, they don't just disappear. They lurk inside on the subconscious level impacting today's choices and decisions.

In this December 17, 2000 dream, God revealed to me that my past was still a real part of my present. Although by then, I was learning to submit to Him, I missed this message, like I did most of the others.

I was changing a baby's diaper. As I walked away momentarily, someone approached the infant. I hurried back to the baby. I remember feeling I needed to protect the child from any wrong desires the person may have had.

I believe this dream reveals my sensitivity to children's vulnerabilities. So I find myself actively protecting children and young or old people who, in my opinion, may be in a precarious position to be taken advantage of by an opportunist. Have you witnessed someone who appeared to be victimized?

There was a time when it appeared to me that a couple of respectful, joyful, good kids, fine young men were being belittled and treated with disrespect while their dignity was being stripped from them. No one, especially not a child should be robbed of their dignity nor treated with disrespect.

Since the incidences occurred in my presence twice, I spoke very forcibly to the adult perpetrator each time. However, could I have done more without making matters worse for the children?

It can feel overwhelming when we have to face past injuries like these and start working through the lies to reveal the truth. At the same time, bringing trauma from darkness to light has now created a path to the healing process for me.

I believe determining what is truth and what is not takes a lot of the sting out of the situation. In my case, finally accepting that I was taken advantage of freed me from much of the weight of shame and guilt I carried. Again, it is all a process. Sometimes I am inclined to pray, Lord I believe, help my unbelief.

What are you dragging along? It's time to be free!

Time of Reflection:

❖ What would God have us to do, situation by situation to support the innocent?

❖ Do you ask Him, or do you turn your head and look the other way?

From Parent to Child - July 4, 2007

I dreamed Larry had gotten or was getting married.

Larry had always said he never wanted to get married, yet he got married in March 2018 to a very lovely but firm young lady, Alisa who most certainly was not going to tolerate unfair criticism.

Their love story was so romantic to me. Larry says he promised the Lord, if you bless me with her, I will change my life. I see evidence of that maturity happening in his life at this time and it brings me great joy. But, regrettably, they separated shortly after they were married.

The awakening: Now I see clearly how our children learn our behaviors—good or bad. Unfortunately, Larry was plagued with my insecurities, my attitude, my argumentative nature, my uncompromising spirit with insensitivity to the feelings of others.

It's highly probable that he learned this negative way of communicating through observing my outbursts. In their marriage, very early on, this behavior cost them dearly.

It is my hope that as he and she grow closer to the Lord, they will choose to overcome the obstacles, and build a joyful, God-fearing marriage relationship either with each other or with someone else who can love, respect and cherish their lives together.

I am hopeful Bill and my relationship will be a better example to Larry than what I demonstrated in his younger years.

From Dreams to *Awakening*!

Your Reflections

From Gifting to Sharing - Gifts and Calling are Without Repentance

In this impactful dream, I believe God was revealing a gift, a talent, a purpose. I was at work and everywhere I went, as I started to write, I felt a great sense of joy and fulfillment. In each instance, when I started writing, it brought a source of joy. This dream was on December 30, 1985.

I started journaling before adolescence. And as far back as I can recall, I've seized every opportunity to pen hope and inspiration to people in my circle of influence.

Joseph (my first husband) shared a similar dream he had that fits here as well. In his dream of April 26, 2009, he saw this bright light coming toward him. As the light got closer, he saw my face within.

He saw large angels surrounding me. I spoke and said, I want to make things right with everyone I may have offended, and I started writing. As I wrote, he said the angels started singing and praising God.

My guess is the rejoicing was related to my on purpose use of the gifting God gave me. Most times I have to pull myself away when I start writing.

In particular, it appears this book has a draw on my spirit like none of the previous manuscripts I've penned. Even when I am not writing, points are being formed in my psyche. May this writing bring glory to God alone, and reach each reader with the "Word" God ordained **specifically** for them through His gifting.

I also hope angels are singing and praising God and that these books will cause "you, the reader" to praise God for how He touches you through them. If your joy of reading is even half as much as my joy of writing, it will be most beneficial.

A time of Reconciliation:

To those unnamed and unknown individuals before whom I may have misrepresented Christ, forgive me please. By the grace of God, I am a new creation in Christ. May the new me have the greater impact on you. May you all not only see Christ in me but feel His love through me and be drawn to Him.

More to reflect upon!

❖ What is your gift?

❖ Is any sin standing in the way of that gift or are you using it on purpose?

From Hope to Desire – the Announcement!

December 1990, I dreamed Larry was a daddy! Boo, my deceased sister came to see the baby. She said she had been gone for three years. Larry was playing with the baby, loving on her.

It appears the Lord used the spirit of my sister Angela (affectionately called Boo) to announce that I was about to be a granny. I shared the dream with mom and she said, "that girl must be pregnant then."

Not only did the Lord send me this announcement, like he did for Abraham and Sarah, Zechariah and Elizabeth, and Joseph & Mary, but He blessed me with the privilege through Tab's mom, Feleciette, to name her. She was named from Acts 9 which I thought had been given me for my future daughter.

Tabitha was a disciple and follower of Christ; always doing good, showing acts of charity and generosity toward others, especially the needy. The Greek name is Dorcas. The name means gazelle, a beautiful, swift, and graceful animal with large, bright eyes.

Our Tabitha has proven to be the daughter I desired. The Lord knitted us together early on. Unlike my example before Larry—of following Vivian, my example before her has been more of following God.

Over the course of her life, I shed many tears and suffered many heart breaks with her. The worst times were those wherein she put high expectations in individuals, who at the time were not able to deliver.

Once she stayed awake all night believing that a promise made would be fulfilled. When I was told about the situation, my heart broke and ached with hers. I could only imagine how devastating that was for a child.

In another instance, as a teen, she made an attempt to pretend as if the disappointment of the moment didn't hurt. The Lord blessed her with a loving, caring always come to the rescue--substitute (good ole Uncle Bernard).

Nonetheless, as they stood there, uncontrollable tears rolled down her cheeks. As I watched, my grief for her was excruciating. I had been there in the lane of disappointment many times over in my own life. I too, had to learn the hard way; we are to put our expectations in God, not in humans.

Yes, her name means graceful and swift. And that she is. Despite that, like all of us, she has experienced not only disappointment, but betrayal and dishonor.

Humans will fail us but God never will. I know God will give her this revelation in His own timing.

Tabitha fully embodies the character and spirit of Dorcas. At a very early age, she was blessed to discover many gifts and talents God instilled in her. She uses those passions to bless not just herself and her livelihood, but others as well. When we leave her stylist chair, we feel not only beautiful, but invigorated too!

God gave me a daughter, not in the traditional way, but in His own special way. He's showing that at times our prayers are answered unconventionally.

It is my hope that you too will recognize those answers God sends in His own way. He truly knows best and only gives us His best! And often He does it in ways that astound us.

Maybe you are longing to have a child in the home and you are hoping to conceive and bear one. Like with Hannah and Elizabeth, God can open the womb; however, be sure to listen for other ways He may be speaking to you about becoming parents of a child or children He has already placed in the world just to be embraced by you.

God continues to show me that whenever I follow Him, there is great fulfillment at the end of the obedience. I believe there is fulfillment for you too.

Something to Consider!

❖ How have you experienced disappointment? Betrayal?

❖ Have you ever made unfulfilled commitments yourself? If yes, what now?

May I suggest to you, make it a habit not to commit to anyone, especially children unless absolutely sure you can fulfill the promise!!!

Your Reflections

_____

_____

_____

_____

_____

_____

_____

_____

_____

_____

_____

_____

_____

_____

_____

_____

_____

_____

_____

_____

_____

_____

From God through a Babe - Out of the mouths of Babes and Sucklings

December 12, 2001--dreamed we were preparing to hold hands and pray. It was about five people. Before we could complete the circle, Tabitha, my ten-year-old granddaughter, began to speak. I said the Lord is speaking.

I became attentive and said in my heart, Tabitha doesn't have this knowledge, this has to be the Lord. By message end, I was positive it was God. However, when I awakened, the words spoken through her had escaped my memory.

Today, I see how God's wisdom through her blesses me time and again. God has used this wisdom to help me become a more mature, balanced, understanding, less abrasive woman. Tab also taught me to dress age appropriate without looking my age (clothing, hair, and lashes too). She says, "just because you are a granny, doesn't mean you have to look like one." Ooch!

That same wisdom has helped Bill and I navigate a new relationship through unchartered waters of trust and honor for each other. She advised us to make good memories saying you have enough bad ones. We are taking her advice and enjoying the new moments and memories.

God spoke through a donkey (Numbers 22:28). What could make us conclude He can not speak through a child (see Matthew 21:16)? Could it be, we know it's truth, yet the truth is not what we want to hear, so we make excuses that give good reason for us to ignore that truth?

I read recently (V. McGee), "if a man keeps rejecting the light (truth), there will come a day when God will withdraw that light altogether." Jesus is truth and light. Light is our Friend. Darkness is simply a cloak for sin, a very costly cover.

"This is the verdict: Light has come into the world, but people loved darkness instead of light because their deeds were evil."

Think this one through!

❖ Is there a babe speaking truths (shining the light) into your life that you have not yet accepted as from our Father? What next?

From Failure to Success – He is the God of Second Chances

Tabitha asked if her room is still clean, she is moving in. When I awakened, I cleaned the room that she uses when she visits. I realize today that God gave me a second opportunity to represent Him better as a parent/granny. This was August 19, 2005.

Bill predicted years before that she would live with me one day but I firmly denied that she would even have that desire. Turns out he was right. After college she moved in. We spent the next six years growing together. I gave my all as a second chance parent, in surrender to Jesus as Lord. I was eager to represent Him well.

I am grateful. We had a lot of relational growth. I learned from her. She learned from me. She was respectful. She obeyed the rules of the house even when she disagreed. We butt heads sometimes too, but with God's help, we resolved conflict quickly. God used our situation to prepare me for living with my husband as a more mature lady.

By now you know that I believe not only is He the God of second chances, but He is a gentleman and the God that doesn't waste anything. He says gather up the fragments that none be lost.

My friend, do you feel like you have wasted your life? With God, what you consider waste can be turned into something beautiful to bless yourself and others—from ashes to beauty, if you let Him. Will you?

A true gentleman will never force himself on you and God is the ultimate gentleman.

Points to Think About!

❖ Is He giving you a second chance in some area of your life? If so, what are you doing with it?

❖ Is He ready to turn your mess into a message?

From Dreams to *Awakening*!

Your Reflections

_____

_____

_____

_____

_____

_____

_____

_____

_____

_____

_____

_____

_____

_____

_____

_____

_____

_____

_____

_____

_____

From My Way to Divine Order, Hand in Hand -- March 19, 2012

Dreamed Bill reached for my hand. I put mine in his and he led. As he walked forward, I placed my feet on his feet and walked. I felt "peace and at ease".

God has an order. Whenever any of us try to change that order, we will run into trouble. God is the head of man. Man is head of his wife. This dream was guidance from God showing me the way to peace in my marriage.

God is helping me get in my lane. And to let He and Bill handle the heavy work. Most times, I am walking alone beside them--not trying to lead!

Furthermore, a few years back, while reading the story of Hannah, I made a statement to God. "Lord, if You give me back my husband, I will give him back to You all the days of our lives together."

Whenever I keep that promise, this peace and ease" is visibly present. When I find myself trying to lead, I sense the unwanted shift in energy.

Think about your closest relationships—are things in order according to God's plan? If not, I can guarantee you are experiencing some level of chaos. Or someone is trying to bite their tongue.

Either way, it can't continue in such a chaotic unhealthy state and mature in love at the same time.

To obtain harmony, I've learned that God's order for relationships is the walk that works.

Are there bumps in the road? Yes, there are. God did not say there would be no rivers, no fires and no storms. BUT He did say He would walk through the river with us and be with us in the fire and the storm.

Points of reflection:

❖ What is He saying to you right now—about any relationship?

❖ Are you surrendering to His divine order or creating your own order?

Vivian Larkin

From Raging Storm to Calm - Refuge from Tornado

What causes family fallouts? Why family? Can family issues be resolved in a loving and peaceful way that benefits all?

God created family. He knew we would see character flaws in each other. He knew we could speak the truth in love to each other. Forgive each other. And keep walking in love, light and harmony. This creates a united front for next generations to follow.

Satan hates families, so he seeks to steal, kill, and destroy the family unit. So instead of listening to God's still small voice, we family members get in our feelings, and we fall prey.

Why do we yield to this enemy? Why do we give up on something so fulfilling as a loving family? What must we do to walk in victory as families?

Not sure why, but I did not write the date of this dream. It was recorded between May 15 and June 14, 1998, where there was a gap in my journaling.

I dreamed I walked out and saw a tornado coming. I ran to cover in a shed, getting down behind something. I was facing the door and a couple of trees. I knew we were in the path of the storm so I assumed trees, shed and me would be destroyed. Yet, I prayed for safety.

The trees never moved but when I sensed the storm had passed, I went out. The storm was over. I saw one of my siblings who was previously estranged. She was laughing and talking with me. In disbelief, I said to myself, she is not angry with me anymore. End of dream.

Mom passed in May 1997. Shortly before that, the family unit started down a path which broke God's heart and would have broken mom's heart too. Somewhere we messed up. Things started going south. Then at a point, I felt an inner tug to let go. Leave it lovingly to God.

This dream, as interpreted by a friend indicated God gave me grace to see the oncoming storm. He gave me wisdom to seek cover as the storm passed over. The covering was in Him and that is why I was untouched by the storm.

Since this sibling and I were lovingly engaging after the storm, God was revealing that the storm was in relation to what we had been going through since mother's illness and death and that harmony would come again.

It seems the Lord confirmed that the decision made to leave it to Him, and to follow peace was the right move. Storms always pass. But what we do or don't do in the midst of them can have far reaching consequences.

The storm in the dream, passed over without

leaving a devastating trail. In our family, there is hope as well. I can see God's hand moving, furthermore, I know He's not done with us! He's working still and I'm partnered with Him. Just trusting to hear and obey the next command.

God gave us individual uniqueness for a reason. One person's difference doesn't make them better or worst, just different. As a family, how can we find ways to harness our differences into a cohesive unit and bring restorative healing and growth for our descendents to follow?

It would give me great joy to see families come together in love and harmony and whip the devil's socks off. Especially my family whom I love dearly. Are you willing to be God's vessel of restoration in your family? I believe to do so would make God smile, therefore I'm all in. He loves relationships, especially family.

Time for reflection!

❖ How is your family doing at this time?

❖ Is there a spirit of unforgiveness that needs to be revealed and uprooted?

❖ What can you do to help establish amiable relationships?

From Dreams to *Awakening*!

Your Reflections

_____

_____

_____

_____

_____

_____

_____

_____

_____

_____

_____

_____

_____

_____

_____

_____

_____

_____

_____

_____

_____

_____

_____

From Ashes to Beauty - Joy and Peace after the Storm

This is two years later, and mom came to me. On July 28, 2000 I dreamed mom asked what I would like for my siblings. Then she gave me a post it note. I wrote "**joy**" and "**peace.**" Immediately afterward, came disharmony between me and several siblings about material things... namely someone driving my vehicle.

In 2006, as I read this dream, I wrote that my priorities were out of order and there was pride. In 2017, I wrote – priorities closer to God's will/way. In 2018 I was led to set up a family fun day at the park.

Sometime before the event took place in 2019, the Lord led me to a scripture in Isaiah "For you shall go out in joy and be led forth in peace; the mountains and the hills before you shall break forth into singing, and all the trees of the field shall clap their hands." I knew this was direction for the outing.

The Lord blessed with an on-site caterer. The next generation chipped in with games and fun stuff (Domonique, Tabitha, Martika and ShyKimeyun). Cousin Jr was our DJ and yours truly, the photographer.

Everything went so well until after the event, we didn't want to leave. It's apparent; the Lord is still fighting for us. We stood around. Talking and expressing how happy we thought the whole gathering had made mom.

A few days later, a photo of mom with a smile on her face resurfaced on my Facebook page bringing me overwhelming joy. I was sure it was confirmation of the joy and peace and LOVE we all experienced that weekend.

Time for More Thinking!

❖ Will you be a vessel of use to God in your family?

❖ Can you see the calm after the storm?

Vivian Larkin

Your Reflections

_____

_____

_____

_____

_____

_____

_____

_____

_____

_____

_____

_____

_____

_____

_____

_____

_____

_____

_____

_____

_____

_____

_____

_____

From death to Life - Living Waters -- March 29, 1998

In this dream, we were gathered at a river. People were putting plants in the water that were coming back to life. I put my plants in and witnessed the same. Later I stepped in the clear water. It reached my calf.

I walked beyond the clear water to the bloody water and I was coming back out of the water when someone said you are so pretty. I said if you think I am pretty, you should see my sister. She is the pretty one. I was thinking of Jessie.

Interpretation through a dear interpreter of dreams – God is blessing me. Without shedding of blood there is no remission of sin. The water represents the life of the spirit. The beauty is in the ways of the Word of the Lord.

Watering plants – plants are my works; other people that I minister to. If the water is applied they come to life. Can be seeds that have been planted in my life, even bad seeds; apply the water to them and they come to life. When I went to the bloody water, it represented knowing that if it could give life to plants, it could do the same for me.

No matter what it is in my life, if I apply the Word and prayer, even if it is withered, life can be restored. People know when you are being blessed. They can see it.

As I continue to launch out into the deep, God continues to reveal seeds I've planted, good and bad seeds. He has grown me significantly--from lukewarm to a state of reverential fear and devotion.

Recently, my nine-year-old god-great grand called to tell me she learned that God made everything and rested on the seventh day. Then she said, I just realized that Sunday is the seventh day. Listen y'all. God was speaking to her. She was listening. Because she was listening, she heard what He said.

This same sweet A'siya had previously told me she didn't like to read. She spent more time on tic-toc and other technological advances than she did reading. I felt led to give her a large book of Bible stories I had purchased many years ago when my grandchildren were small. I asked her and mom to read it together. They were encouraged to call me with any questions.

She went on to explain that God made the sky and the stars and exclaimed how happy it makes her to learn these things. I asked where she learned them, she said from the book you gave me. This was good fruit manifesting. It warmed my heart. It made my day!

On the same day, my granddaughter called and told me she worked at the "new here, connect here" booth at church. A great fit for her personality.

She also indicated she felt led to go with the First Lady and others to take gifts and love to the young teens at an orphanage in Tennessee. I believe God will truly bless the young ladies to relate to her since she is quite young herself. She too is hearing God! What a joy.

Determine what you want your future to look like and start planting good seeds now. The past is the past. We can not go back to change it. On the other hand, we can better our tomorrows by the choices we make today. I am a fond believer that "all choices have consequences."

Think about this!

❖ What seeds are you planting?

Vivian Larkin

Your Reflections

_____
_____
_____
_____
_____
_____
_____
_____
_____
_____
_____
_____
_____
_____
_____
_____
_____
_____
_____
_____
_____
_____
_____

In sickness and in health, from insecure to security - April 20, 2019

Mom and dad had separated before dad's demise but he could come by for food and conversation whenever he chose to. The sober dad was kind, sometimes funny and loved to dance like Big Mama (his mama).

Mom tried taking care of him after the surgery. Eventually, because of the unbearable pain he was experiencing, he was admitted into a nursing facility.

In a dream of mom and dad on April 20, 2019, the three of us were talking. I did not remember the conversation upon arising, but I could still feel their warmth.

We walked out the house, and then I turned back for something. On my way out the second time, dad met me. I followed him out a different door. We agreed that the door was not secure. End of dream.

I am glad they were together in this dream and I am grateful for the warmness I felt in their presence.

In addition, may the Lord help me choose the secure doors He opens and turn quickly from those He shuts.

Reflection Time!

❖ Is there someone you can express unconditional love to right now?

Vivian Larkin

From Fear to Faith - Letting Go and Trusting God

I was flying in the sky, trying to guide myself. Hopeful I would land safely. Suddenly, I chose to trust God. Then I began to enjoy the flight. I actually started floating.

I felt confident He had prepared a place for my landing. When it was over, I landed safely, kinda floated into water. I was standing on both feet, and the landing was smooth. Dream of December 6, 2000.

Scripture says "but those who trust in the Lord will find new strength. They will soar high on wings like eagles. They will run and not grow weary. They will walk and not faint."

Trusting Him feels like floating through life, one moment at a time, one situation or circumstance at a time! Knowing, "everything in life is already done, when I do life God's way.

Forget trying to make things happen. Just honor God and let His will be done. In His timing.

Think on this!

❖ How do you encourage yourself to trust God in the tough times?

❖ Why should we trust Him in the storms?

From Judge to Witness -- Bearing Witness to the Truth

How did you first come to know Jesus? In this vision of October 6, 2001, I was telling others how I heard of the goodness of Christ. It was through my sponsor while in the military and it made me question my relationship with Christ.

She was always talking about what God was doing in her life. I began to wonder why He was not so active in mine. I was impelled to find the difference between her religion and mine.

In the vision, it dawned on me that I must tell people of God's goodness in my life. So I began. This dream confirmed what actually happened during my military career in the late seventies.

In addition, it also revealed that I need to be a witness like she was so that others may be drawn to the Father just like I was drawn through her witness.

This book is one of the ways I am witnessing of His goodness in my life.

More Reflections!

❖ In what ways are you reaching others with the gospel?

Vivian Larkin

From Frown to Smile - The Joy of the Lord

I saw myself standing there with a slight smile on my face, looking radiant and beautiful. I remember turning my thoughts toward the Lord, then the smile graced my face. This was March 4 or 5, 2002

At that time in my life, I was a person so somber about everything that my sister Jessie told me, "You need to lighten up sis, you are way too serious." By the same token, many co-workers told me I "had" an unapproachable look.

I can **NOT** represent God in a way that draws people to Him if I appear unapproachable and overly serious. This dream appears to be instructional and directional for the fulfillment of purpose.

Smiling more is a commitment I have made to myself. And I have found that by affirming the power and presence of the Lord in my life, I can smile radiantly because at that moment, I know He loves me, He has my back and as long as I continue to do my best to honor Him, everything is working out for good.

Are there moments when I don't feel this way, you bet? But when I acknowledge that feeling of fear, I do like David, I start encouraging myself by remembering what He has already done. I start being grateful.

Do you express gratitude on a regular? Or like me, do you need a tender reminder here and there?

Reflections!

❖ Do you make it a habit of sharing the joy of the Lord with others?

❖ In what ways do you exhibit that joy?

Vivian Larkin

Your Reflections

_____

_____

_____

_____

_____

_____

_____

_____

_____

_____

_____

_____

_____

_____

_____

_____

_____

_____

_____

_____

_____

_____

_____

_____

_____

_____

From Pride to Honor - Stand and See this great thing - November 20, 2005

God loves us and He has great plans for our lives. "For I know the plans I have for you declares the Lord; plans to prosper you and not to harm you; plans to give you hope and a future" (Jeremiah 29:11). God created us and knows what brings us the greatest fulfillment.

We take our Range Rover to a Range Rover dealer for repairs. Why? Because we believe as the maker, they know more about the car than our neighborhood Chevy dealer.

Likewise, as our Creator, God knows exactly what we need to gain the greatest fulfillment in our lives. This means we should run to Him for guidance on how to live our best lives.

In this dream, someone told me, "The Lord is going to do great things concerning you." I replied, He just gave me that word, "now therefore stand and see this great thing which the Lord will do before your eyes."

❖ God has wooed me to Himself. In spite of many bad choices that could have landed me in the hospital or the grave, He's kept me healthy and alive.

❖ The Lord has resurrected a marriage that I had begun to believe had no hope of reconciliation. Do we still have struggles? Yes, but He's got us.

❖ He is blessing me to pen this book and blessed me to be very close to being debt free again.

These are milestones. I eagerly expect and anticipate all the other "great things He is going to do concerning me and 'us'". I know He has only just begun. He's never been the problem. I was.

Reflections!

❖ Are you, too, the one hindering progress in your life?

From Disconnect to Connection – October 8, 2005

Dreamed Larry connected with Tabitha. Then he sat beside me. No words. Later I got up and walked around the building seven times. End of dream

In gratitude to God for this visualized connection, I was inspired to follow the leading from it and walk around a representation of Larry seven times. For I knew God could work good out of my messed up role as a mom. The way I handled child rearing was not a surprise to Him.

Fathers are the glory of their children (Proverbs 17). I know for a fact that Larry's three children love him, love him, love him. But for years, Larry was absent in each of their lives or made commitments he was unable to keep. Was it partially because I set a poor example as a mom and because he and I had a disconnected relationship?

I clearly remember having labor pains on December 20th, 1967, and I recall giving birth naturally in the colored section of Sam's Hospital. The next thing I can remember explicitly was waking up and looking directly into those little eyes staring up at me. It was love at first sight. My heart was smitten. I savored the moment. Then grief came as my mind went to the commitment I made to Mrs. W.

Ms. W. was my beloved teacher. She and her

husband wanted children but were unable to conceive. Since I wanted my baby to have a good home with a mother and a father, I committed to give my little one to her at birth. After looking into those eyes and falling in love, I could no longer keep that commitment and I pondered for days how I would be able to share that news with her.

I finally determined there was no easy way. So I wrote her a note and shared how much I loved him. She responded in kind. She was so excited for me. They still wanted Larry, BUT at the same time, she had become pregnant and understood if I chose to keep him. I am telling you, God always has a plan and He is always purposeful.

Regardless of what the world says, the Lord's plan is always best! When we disregard God's plan for marital relationships, for sex, for parenting, even for communicating, our children suffer most. I have also learned that even when one or both parents are missing, fortunately God is still purposeful. He can bring good out of bad situations.

The Awakening (sixteen years after this dream) Oct 19, 2021: Proverbs tells us that the walls erected through offense are not easily broken. Did I offend Larry as a child? Hindsight tells me definitely so. Just as I was offended by the shortcomings of my dad, I caused offense in my child because of my foolish ways as a mom and as a wife.

It came to me that this dream definitely has a correlation to the impenetrable Jericho walls Joshua faced when they entered the Promised Land. God gave very specific instructions on what to do to cause the walls to collapse (Joshua 6). This I believe is what He did for me in this dream.

I'm thinking the impenetrable walls had been built up sub-consciously as a way of self-protect for Larry. I know all too well about self-protect. At God's appointed time, those walls around Larry's heart must fall down.

After the collapse, Larry will have that fatherly connection not only with Tabitha, but with his second born--Marquis and his youngest—DeVonn. Plus true mom/son connection will be restored between he and I without a word.

The dream assures me that the day will come when, without words, we will have that reconciliation because He is the God of reconciliation.

Time for Feedback

❖ Have you experienced such a breakthrough?

❖ Any suggestions how to help others, including me, bridge that gap?

Your Reflections

_____

_____

_____

_____

_____

_____

_____

_____

_____

_____

_____

_____

_____

_____

_____

_____

_____

_____

_____

_____

_____

_____

_____

_____

_____

From Secret to Breakthrough. From Darkness to Light – No means No

I was telling Tabitha to say "no" to inappropriate affection toward her.

NOTE to self upon awakening: Be sure she understands. The Lord is with me. I committed it to prayer that God would help me follow His lead. Dream of October 8, 2005.

At first, I did not know how to approach the subject but felt courage to just do it. I must have told her and her friends a thousand times that if it doesn't feel right when someone tries to touch them, it isn't right. You must tell somebody.

After she got older, I shared with her about the molestation I experienced as a child. About a year ago, she asked me to speak to a friend of hers who had been through a similar experience. She was having a really hard time coping.

Tab said, she felt that I could relate to the friend and the friend to me. She was right! We talked. We were able to connect and during the process we bore one's another pain and cried together.

Dear reader, what is your story? Don't be afraid to use it to bless others. If God allowed it, He can use it to help someone else navigate through life.

It is satan who wants us to keep our pain secret, because he knows when we shine light on it, it will be beneficial to us and others along the way. Remember, he is the father of lies and he comes to steal, kill, and destroy. He has stolen enough of my joy and peace. Yours too I hope! I encourage you to let there be light. Take that power back. Make it known and start your healing process.

Deserves Serious Thought!

❖ How can your experiences benefit others?

❖ Ask God to show you how and when to share?

Promotion Comes from God, Tuesday, February 1, 2011

Dreamed Plant Manager called me on the phone. She asked if I was standing and I said I am sitting. She informed me that they had selected me for the level 20 OSS and that they are finalizing paperwork. I was elated.

When I awakened, I said oh, it was a just a dream. Then the Spirit reminded me it was not "just" a dream, it was the Father "speaking to me in dreams and visions."

The day before God had ministered...promotion comes neither from the east, nor the south, nor from the west, but God is the judge. He was confirming His word to me. Later in the day, it came to me that I have passed the test, met the requirement and the Lord has given me a promotion.

That promotion entails "spiritual first" ...eye hath not seen, ear hath not heard, neither has entered into the heart of man, the things which God has prepared for those who love Him, but God has revealed them to us by His spirit.

In my spirit is the knowledge that promotion includes redeemed relationships--in marriage, in family, with friends; promotion at work, greater opportunities to honor God with the door opening that He has purposed.

The Lord blessed me with that job promotion a year

later. Then three years after that, another. All along the way, He has been blessing with redeemed relationships including my marriage.

God is always working. Seems it has taken me forever to listen and take action. Please don't follow my path, be a better listener than I was. And if you are on that path, make a choice to get off and seek God. When we seek Him, we will find Him.

Reflections!

❖ Are you seeking God?

❖ Are you recognizing Him in your life?

From Dreams to *Awakening*!

Your Reflections

_____

_____

_____

_____

_____

_____

_____

_____

_____

_____

_____

_____

_____

_____

_____

_____

_____

_____

_____

_____

_____

_____

_____

_____

Love of a Mother Endures - July 2nd, 2008

Mom was combing my hair. Then she told me to go get her purse. Seems we had been in this place and left. I went back and asked the ladies if there was an extra purse there. They gave me the purse.

I looked in it to see if mom' ID was in there but all I saw was a roll of money and one other thing. I do not recall what the other item was. But I do recall thinking that the reason mom has no ID is because she is no longer alive.

In real life, I never remember mom combing my hair although I am sure she did. Yet this dream caused me to feel the warm and soothing love of her touch. This is something in which I am sure we can all relate.

Reflections!

❖ May I ask here, if you still have mom or dad, why not take the time to brush their hair without the rush? Or do something else that speaks their love language? Help them feel your love and appreciation for all or just something special they did over the years.

❖ If you are a parent, will you put that extra touch into helping your child feel truly loved and special today?

From darkness to Light - Obedience is better than Sacrifice - May 17, 2009

Dreamed the Bible fell off the bed. I heard pages turning. I picked it up. It was Revelations. At the top of the page I saw "obey". I read but couldn't recall the words. Later in my spirit came the words, "thou are clothed with a clothing".

God clothes His children with salvation and righteousness (right standing in Christ) as indicated in Psalms 131. Further, we are instructed in Colossians to cloth ourselves with compassion, kindness, humility, gentleness and patience....over all, we are to put on love.

God does His part when we confess Jesus as Savior. We get to choose to do our part. For me, that became a greater reality after I made Him Lord. Today, I recognize that it's a choice I get to make over and over again.

I can see where the Lord made the message of this dream crystal clear. And He is summing up the whole matter for me. Simply walk as a child of God through obedience. Obey what I understand to be Truth.

It reminds me of when I was eight, I was attempting to read the Bible at my grandparents. Grandpa saw me. He said, "Gal, if you ain't gonna live by it, don't read it." I was trying to read it like a book, from front to back. I was in the Old Testament. So I did put it down because I couldn't understand the words.

I now know the veil was there. The Word declares that the veil was split in half when Christ died for our sins, but the veil remains to those who are reading the Word without Christ as Savior.

When I confessed Jesus and picked it up again years later, I thought I was taking heed to what Pa said. I was wrong about that. I was getting the knowledge but understanding alluded me because my own desires were in control. Knowledge puffs up, but love edifies.

Instead of applying what I was learning to my life, I tried to get others to apply it to theirs. Today I am aware that God's Word is His love letter to us, not our weapon to beat others across the head with what we have learned. When we learn to love, we can edify others. We must show compassion before we offer advice. For we are to be doers of the Word, and not hearers only, deceiving ourselves....he who looks into the perfect law of liberty and continues in it, and is not a forgetful hearer but a doer of the work, this one will be blessed in what he does (James). The change had to begin with me, and then others could be drawn through what He was doing in me.

God's way can not be subjected to our methods. I know that very well now. He is the light and He is continually shining light on our paths. Has this light shown in your life yet? May He help us walk in the light.

He is not looking for anything we have to offer if our heart is cold toward Him. He wants our devoted hearts.

To obey is better than sacrifice.

Serious Reflection!

❖ When others see your walk, are they drawn to Christ?

Vivian Larkin

Your Reflections

From Death to Life - One Plants, Another Waters, God Gives the Increase

Dreamed I was planting flowers. They were colorful. I felt the leaves. They were thick and strong like tropical plants.

Once the sun came through, as if they were reaching for the sun, they started opening up more and more right before my eyes. There were so many brilliant colors. I was elated with joy at the beauty surrounding me. And I was eager to plant more! This dream was February 15, 2019.

This dream leads me to daresay it's about winning souls. And now that I am taking heed to His guidance, as I live out life following His lead, He is glorified. As my life touches the lives of others, they too blossom and bring Him glory.

One plants, another waters but He gives the increase. Can you think of a time when you just knew you were supposed to be a blessing to someone, even if it was a simple smile or a kind word; but you talked yourself out of it?

Minutes after the opportunity passed, you then wished you had followed the lead. This has happened to me too many times. May we hear and obey, hear and obey, hear and obey.

From Man's Grasp to God's Control - April 27, 2021

Dreamed Bill and I were traveling by car. He was driving. We were having good conversation. Seems Aunt Mary was in the back seat. Then at some point, Bill stopped steering, but the car was still moving. I had concern and asked for Auntie's opinion.

Auntie laughed her usual laugh. Then she said she felt we were riding with Jesus!!! Next part of dream, we sat down at a table to eat. Seemed to be a fourth person but don't know who.

Auntie has such a welcoming spirit. She truly loves. She exudes--family unity!

From Blindness to Sight - October 6, 2021

Auntie Cat and I were talking on the phone. She said, can't we see what God is doing? Can't we see what God is revealing?

As the dream indicates, can we not see what God is doing and revealing? I was so blind. God is and has been speaking to me for a long time. He's revealed pitfalls to avoid. He showed me that I would defy His will.

He has shown me what it looks like with me in control versus how it is with Him in control. He revealed times when I would yield and obey and times when I would choose not to.

As this dream indicates, may our eyes open to see the hand of God at work!

When Auntie worships God, if the anointing doesn't move you, you may want to check your pulse!

The Love of a Father – November 15, 2021

Dad came to see me and gave me a big, warm embrace. We communicated for a while and I asked him to let's take a ride to Miami to see his brother Benjamin. I awakened filled with joy. That joy carried me through a busy week.

Did my Redeemer, my Deliver send this heart warming embrace because I am **"finally"** awakening and fully understanding "Father knows best"?

From Dreams to *Awakening*!

Your Reflections

_____

_____

_____

_____

_____

_____

_____

_____

_____

_____

_____

_____

_____

_____

_____

_____

_____

_____

_____

_____

_____

_____

_____

_____

Vivian Larkin

A Look Back

I have shared some of the most intimate details about God's unrelenting pursuit of my heart and my ultimate full surrender to His call. I am grateful to be experiencing an overwhelming awakening as I pen many of His messages in this writing! He that has ears, let Him hear what the spirit is saying!

Know that my unjustifiable belief that my plans were better than His caused me to make terrible choices. Those choices prolonged the chase and brought more harm than good for me. Our God still did not give up on me. He will not give up on you either.

Where I am now (willing AND choosing to honor His heart) is not where I was without Him (angry, prideful, controlling, ashamed, full of guilt, distrusting...). My life is becoming a living testimony to His relentless love.

We need to know, God is for us and not against us! He gave us free will on purpose. He also left a guide book (the Holy Bible) on the most appropriate ways to use that will. It's up to us to use the manual and to train our children to use it.

Most importantly, don't be like I was, choosing the parts that suited my agenda. May you recognize His never ending, unconditional love for you. May your response be conducive to His will.

Let me reemphasize, God is the One True Gentleman

and I can not say that enough. Although some of our choices break His heart because they bring trouble to us or to others, He will not take that choice away from us.

The essence of this book is: I tried to control my own life, but through vivid dreams, God kept pursuing me. While in a hog-pen of a situation, I started listening and learning obedience. I began to change, and thereafter, my situations began to change. The Lord helped me see, I can only walk in victory when I walk with Him.

The Lord wants me to remember that He led me all this way...to humble me, to test me and to know what was in my heart, whether I would keep His commandments or not. (Deuteronomy 8:2)

I say to you, regardless of His mode of communication, God still speaks. He uses dreams and visions, His written Word, and the Holy Spirit living on the inside of us. Other sources are people, nature, angelic beings, and music. He even used a donkey once, so there is no end to the ways He speaks. He is the Creator. Everything must bow to Him.

I know there is work still to be done in me and He continues to speak messaging to me to work ungodly characteristics out of my life. I am grateful for that. I continue on this journey with the rest of us. Difference for me now, I have awakened!

When I'm at my lowest, I still hear Him best through song and music. He is the living God after all! He recently said to me, "I will stay close to you (Vivian), instructing and teaching you along the pathway for your life.

"I will advise you along the way and lead you forth with My eyes as your guide. So don't make it difficult, don't be stubborn when I take you where you have not been before. Don't make me tug you and pull you along," (Psalm 32:8-10 TPT).

And He's speaking to you too dear reader! May you be inspired to hear what He is speaking to you! Taste and see that the Lord is good. Blessed is the one who takes refuge in Him!"

"Awake thou that sleepest, and arise...and Christ shall give thee light."*~Ephesians 5:14~*

From Dreams to *Awakening*!

AUTHOR Vivian Larkin was born to Alonza Lee and Clara (Searcy) Alexander in the small town of Reynolds, Georgia. They lived in Junction City, a quaint little town west of Reynolds where her dad was employed, and her mother, a homemaker, and happy mom of ten.

Her father who had to leave school after third grade to work, taught her the importance of education by whipping her "hinny" every morning until she made a willing choice to get on the school bus. Once the decision was made to stop being stubborn and go to school, she started liking it and soon began to excel. Reading, writing, and English, were her favorite subjects in school, which she still enjoys today.

As a result of her love for reading and the quest of finding her Prince Charming she would save every penny until she could order "Love Stories," "True Stories," and all the other fabricated tales of finding love and living happily ever after. After she came to know Jesus, she realized these were fairy tales; however, she didn't recognize how those beliefs had settled in her spirit. So when she met her husband, Bill, who "treated her like a queen," she knew her prince charming had arrived. "Just like I was determined not to get on the bus, I blatantly went heart first even after hearing God say wait a minute."

From Dreams to *Awakening*!

She is an Army veteran, wife, mother, grandmother, great-grandmother, and a retired US Postal worker.

Although she was introduced to Jesus at an early age, she didn't make Him her Lord until she faced the hog pen of life in 1999.

This is her first book about God's relentless pursuit of her heart and how He never gave up on her even when she turned her back on Him.

"This has been an awakening for me and
continues to be so..."
~ Vivian Larkin~

Vivian Larkin

From Dreams to *Awakening*!

CPSIA information can be obtained
at www.ICGtesting.com
Printed in the USA
BVHW041422280422
635622BV00016B/566

9 781946 683427